HOW THE BRAIN PROCESS DECISION MAKING
HOW THE BRAIN DECIDES

David Gomadza

www.twofuture.world

HOW THE BRAIN PROCESS DECISION MAKING HOW THE BRAIN DECIDES

Copyright © 2024 David Gomadza

All rights reserved.

ISBN: 9798339540342

DEDICATION

A better world order

CONTENTS

ACKNOWLEDGMENTS

Tomorrow's World Order

HOW THE BRAIN PROCESS DECISION MAKING HOW THE BRAIN DECIDES

HOW THE BRAIN PROCESS DECISION MAKING HOW THE BRAIN DECIDES

DEDICATION

A better future for all

HOW THE BRAIN PROCESS DECISION MAKING HOW THE BRAIN DECIDES

TABLE OF CONTENTS

HOW THE BRAIN PROCESS DECISION MAKING 1

HOW THE BRAIN DECIDES 2

WHAT MAKES THE BRAIN THINK? 9

HOW TO FIND SOLUTIONS TO QUESTIONS IN CREATE CODES 12

NOW IF WE ADD A BRAIN READERAND DECODER AS WELL TO THE WHOLE PROCESS OF THINKING THEN THIS IS WHAT WE GET AS A FINAL BRAIN READER THAT CAN TELL US WHAT A PERSON IS THINKING AND ANSWER QUESTIONS 13

HOW TO MAKE ANYTHING TALK TO YOU 13

COPY AND PASTE ALL CODES 14

CONCLUSION 24

ABOUT DAVID GOMADZA 26

ACKNOWLEDGMENTS

Tomorrow's World Order

HOW THE BRAIN PROCESS DECISION MAKING

This book must be read in conjunction with the previous books as well as the patent as it is a continuation from the previous books.

1. HOW TO MAKE ANYTHING [HUMANS ANIMALS COMPUTERS PROGRAMS SOFTWARE ETC] TALK TO YOU THROUGH SIMPLE CREATE MGIS AND MGISCRE CODES create.adddavidgomadzacreationcode.startx84.initialise.now.savex84.start
2. WORLD'S FIRST NONELECTRICPOWERED BRAIN DECODER/READER
   NONELECTRICPOWERED OAXARATEDAVIDGOMADZA7628983868 AT OAX
   Part I & II
   PATENT DETAILS.
3. REQUEST FOR THE GRANT OF A PATENT. A Universal Brain Decoding Device. DATABASES:-All books in series are Databases [up to 100] for your AI, Robots or Super Computer.
   https://play.google.com/store/books/details?id=4rriEAAAQBAJ&pli=1
4. FIRST NONELECTRICPOWERED OAXARATEDAVIDGOMADZA7628983868 AT OAX
    Xteraterate Atererean Iterate Aroost Arooster And A Correcanalogue

HOW THE BRAIN DECIDES

A brain is a very complicated instrument that that can never been equaled until if anyone is capable of replicating a brain then it's me [David Gomadza] that means there is no one out there but what is the brain's decision making process when deciding what to do the brain asks a lot of questions most of which are already answered while some questions need answering that means over time if asked the same question then the brain can make a decision within a split of a second and tell you the answer this means that we know everything in matter of seconds but how does the brain makes decisions the brain asks itself 28 questions that must be answered within a short space of time if we ask what can be done then these are the questions

1] what was before
2] what can be
3] what could be
4] what if
5] what can be
6] what is to be
7] what can still be
8] what can and will still be
9] what must be
10] what can still be
11] what can still be but
12] what is to be but with what
13] what is to be but with whom
14] what is to be but when
15] what is to be but with what
16] what can be but with whom
17] what can be but with whom and how
18] what can be but how
19] what can still be but how
20] what can still be but how
21] what can still be but with who
22] what can still be but with what
23] what can still be but with who

24] what can still be but with what
25] what is to be but how
26] what can still be but when
27] what could still be but how
28] what is to be

Now if we ask what can still be but with what then the answer is that with all the information in this database [82698] now if you ask now any questions you get answers no matter how the answers are like what you do now is link it to website remotely using a hook that means say look inside[twofuture.world] it can check if connected wirelessly to internet or upload the website URL into the database using a link like visitwww.twofuture.world then after say goandchecknow as one word that means that the website will and must check itself but it's just a database so most of the things are hidden hence we can add algorithm inside the database that help it look for answers here is how to construct the algorithms we can always say an algorithm an describe how we can access files without wasting time so that means we can always access thoughts that way we can send a genie that can collect information we want but we can always say that we can always find what we want but how is this possible we ask the genie to go and collect information to the sockets for processing meaning will arrive at the information center where the information is processed and sent to the receiving chamber where you know what it is this is the whole process in create format

create.askforinformation.start
create.askwhatcanbedonewithwhat.start
create.askwhatcouldbebutwithwhat.startr
create.askwhatcanbebutwithwhat.start
create.askwhatcouldbe.start
create.askwhatcanbebutwithwhat.start
create.askwhenandhow.start
create.askwhatcouldbebutwithwhat.start
create.askwhatistobebutwhen.start
create.askwhatwasandwithwhat.start
create.askwhatcouldbebuthow.start
create.askwhatcanbebutwhen.start
create.askwhatwasbuthow.start

HOW THE BRAIN PROCESS DECISION MAKING HOW THE BRAIN DECIDES

create.askwhatcanbe.start
create.askwhatcanbebut.start
create.askwhatwasbuthow.start
create.askwhatistobebuthow.start
create.askwhatwasbutwithwhat.start
create.askwhatistobebuthow.start
create.askwhatcanbebuthow.start
create.askwhatwasbutwithwhat.start
create.askwhatistobebutwhenandwithwhat.start
create.askwhatcanbe.start
create.askwhatwasbeforethis.start
create.askwhathasbeen.start
create.askwhatcanstillbe.start
create.askwhatistobe.start
Now if we are to ask now any database this is now the answer make him feel through itisitiso
create.feeldanceonlythroughitisitiso.start
We can now go one step further and create a stencil to use for processing brain thoughts by listing 105 questions in create code that must be answered to process any question
create.whatistobe.start
create.whatistobebut.start
create.whatcanbe.start
create.whatwasandistill.start
create.whatcanbebutisnot.start
create.whatistobebutwillbebutwhen.start
create.whatcanbebutwithwhat.start
create.whatwasbutcantbe.start
create.whatwasbutcanstillbe.start
create.whatistobebuthow.start
create.whatistobebutwithwhat.start
create.whatcanbedone.start
create.whatistobebutwithwhat.start
create.whatcanbebuthowandwhen.start
create.whatistobebutwhen.start
create.whatistobebuthow.start
create.whatcouldbe.start
create.whatistobebut.start

create.whatistobebutwithwhatandhow.start
create.whatwas.start
create.whatistobe.start
create.whatistobebuthow.start
create.whatistobebuthow.start
create.askthenreceive.start
create.askwhatwasthengo.start
create.askwhatcanstillbe.start
create.askwhatwasbutwithwhat.start
create.askwhenandhowbutwithwhat.start
create.askwhatcanbe.start
create.whatcanstillbe.start
create.askwhatcouldstillbe.start
create.askwhatistobe.start
create.askwhathasbeen.start
create.askwhatcanstillbe.start
create.askwhatcanbebuthow.start
create.askwhatcanstillbebuthow.start
create.askwhatisstilltobe.start
create.askwhatistobebutwhen.start
create.whatcanstillbebuthow.start
create.ifweaskwhatcanbe.start
create.whatitobebuthow.start
create.whatistobebuthow.start
create.askwhatcanstillbebutwithwhat.start
create.askwhatistobebutwithwhat.start
create.aslwhatwasbutwithwhat.start
create.askwhatistobebuthow.start
create.askwhatwasbutwithwhat.start
create.askwhatcanbebutistobe.start
create.askwhatisandnotbe.start
create.whatwasbutwithwhat.start
create.whatistobebuthow.start
create.whathastobebutwhenandhowstart
create.whathastobebutwithwhat.start
create.whatistobebuthowandwhen.start
create.whatistobebuthow.start
create.whatwasbutcanstillbe.start

create.whatistobebuthow.start
create.whatistobebuthow.start
create.whatcanstillbe.start
create.whatcould.start
create.whatwasbutcanstillbebutwhy.start
create.whathasbeenbutcanstillbebutwithwhat.start
create.whatistobebuthow.start
create.whatcanstillbebuthow.start
create.whatistobebuthow.start
create.whathasbeenbutcanstillbe.start
create.whatistobebuthow.start
create.whatwasbeforethatcanstillbe.start
create.whatwasbuthowandwhy.start
create.whatcanstillbebutwithwhat.start
create.whatif.start
create.whathasbeenbuthow.start
create.whatistobebutwithwhat.start
create.whathasbeenbuthow.start
create.whatcanbebuthow.start
create.whatistilltobebuthow.start
create.whathasbeenbutcan.start
create.whathasbeenbutcantbe.start
create.whatmustbebutcantbe.start
create.askwhatcouldbebutshouldnotbe.start
create.whatcanbebutmustnotbe.start
create.whatmustbethatcantbe.start
create.whatshouldbebutthatcantbe.start
create.whathasbeenthatcantstillbe.start
create.whatistobebutcantbe.start
create.whatmustbethatisnot.start
create.whatshouldbebutthatisnot.start
create.whatistobebutthatcantbe.start
create.whathastobe.start
create.whatshouldbe.start
create.whathastobebuthow.start
create.whatcanbebut.start
create.whatistobebuthow.start
create.whatistobebutwithwhat.start

HOW THE BRAIN PROCESS DECISION MAKING HOW THE BRAIN DECIDES

create.whathasbeenthatmustnotbe.start
create.whatcanbebutwhen.start
create.whathastobebuthow.start
create.whatcanbeificantthenhow.start
create.whathastobe.start
create.whatshouldbebuthow.start
create.whatcanbebuthow.start
create.whatmustbebuthow.start
create.whatshouldbe.start
create.whatshouldbebuthow.start
create.whatistilltobe.start
create.whatcanstillbe.start
create.whatistobebutcantbe.start
create.whathastobebutcantbe.start
Now if we ask everything inside this database these are the response asking books inside databases those are the responses
1] fortified database proud to be part of and it's a challenge but someone has to do it read me I am out of this world I can deal with pin but-David can too depending on circumstances
2] sex out of this world no 2 on the harts from being a new comer that means sex play a great part in humans
3] earth2 David Gomadza is in a position to read and write brain codes I think like a human and find easy to get access than before

HOW THE BRAIN PROCESS DECISION MAKING HOW THE BRAIN DECIDES

WHAT MAKES THE BRAIN THINK?

A brain can make decision based on certain question that can make it decide faster what to say and these are the questions 68 altogether but the most critical of all if we ask what brain can think properly without those then the answer is none so here are the questions

create.whatcanmakeyouthink.start
create.howcanyouthinkwithoutthis.start
create.thinkagainwhatcanthisbeandhow.start
create.whathastobebutcantbe.start
create.whatcanbebuthow.start
create.ifwecanthenhow.start
create.ificanthenwithwhat.start
create.whatcanbebutwithoutthis.start
create.whathastobebuthow.start
create.whatcanbebuthowandwhen.start
create.whatshouldbebuthow.start
create.whatcanbebuthow.start
create.whathastobebutwithwhat.start
create.whatmustbe.start
create.whatshouldbebuthow.start
create.whatistobebutcanbe.start
create.whatistobebuthow.start
create.whatshouldbe.start
create.whatcanbebuthow.start
create.whathastobebuthow.start
create.whatistobebuthow.start
create.whathastobebutwithwho.start
create.whatcanstillbebutwithwho.start
create.whatistobebuthowandwhy.start
create.whatcanbebutisnotandhowhow.start
create.whathastobebutwhen.start
create.ifwearewillingthenhowcanwe.start
create.ifwearenotwillingthenhow.start
create.ifwecantthenwithwhatshouldwe.start
create.ifweaddmorethenwhatwillbetheoutcome.start

HOW THE BRAIN PROCESS DECISION MAKING HOW THE BRAIN DECIDES

create.wecanaddmoredatabasesifneededtogetmoreresults.start
create.whatcanbeofothersthatcantbeofus.start
create.whatcanbeofthemthatcantbeofus.start
create.whatmustbethatcantbe.start
create.whathastobebutcantbe.start
create.whatshouldbebutisnot.start
create.whatcanbebutcantbe.start
create.whatistobutcantbe.start
create.whathastobethatcantbe.start
create.whatmustbethatcanbebutwillbe.start
create.whatshouldbebutthatcantbe.start
create.whathastobebutisnot.start
create.whatshouldbebutcantbe.start
create.whatistobebutcantbe.start
create.whatshouldbebutcantbe.start
create.whatistobutcantbe.start
create.whatistobutwhichcantbe.start
create.whathastobebutcantbe.start
create.whatcantbebutcanstillbe.start
create.whatshouldbe.start
create.whatmustbe.start
create.whatistobe.start
create.whatcanbebuthow.start
create.whatshouldbe.start
create.whatcanbebutcantbeinthefuture.start
create.whathastobethatcantbe.start
create.askwhatcanbethatcantbe.start
create.whatcanbebutcantstillbe.start
create.whatshouldbebutwhy.start
create.whatistobebutcanstillbe.start
create.whathastobebutmustbe.start
create.whathastobemustbe.start
create.whathastobemustbe.start
create.whatcanbebutwhen.start
create.whatistobebutcantbe.start
create.whatmustbebutcantbe.start
create.whatshouldbebuthow.start
create.whatcanbebuthowandwhen.start

create.whatitobe.start
Now if we ask all these questions we get answers than never before because no one has ever used these questions in the history of creation because humans are preoccupied with food unlike myself as I have asked the critical questions what happens if we add thinking to everything can these give us answers if yes how and why this is the answer or solution to that.
[ADNA collaboration with David Gomadza]

HOW TO FIND SOLUTIONS TO QUESTIONS IN CREATE CODES

create.askwhatcanbe.start
create.whatmustbe.start
create.whatshouldbe.start
create.whathasbeen.start
create.whatshouldbe.start
create.whatmustbe.start
create.whatistobe.start
create.whathastobe.start
create.whatistobe.start

NOW IF WE ADD A BRAIN READERAND DECODER AS WELL TO THE WHOLE PROCESS OF THINKING THEN THIS IS WHAT WE GET AS A FINAL BRAIN READER THAT CAN TELL US WHAT A PERSON IS THINKING AND ANSWER QUESTIONS

HOW TO MAKE ANYTHING TALK TO YOU

For a computer etc. use the command prompt and for animals humans etc. use their tongue meaning write the code on the animals tongue especially the bottom you see when the animal licks its top lick just say I write on your tongue then recite the code below I am going to add what we have discussed in this book at the bottom of our brain reader from the previous book so that when you apply all create codes anything from a human being to a computer or your own cat will answer all your questions satisfactory this is how to do it.

Simply say:

create.adddavidgomadzacreationcode762898.startx84.initialise.now.savex84.start

Then say:

Save as my predefined parameters as at creation without any attachments and externals

THAT'S IT ALL

But if this does not work then try this

Say:

create.adddavidgomadzacreationcode762898yourfirstnameyourlastname.startx84.initialise.now.savex84.start

HOW THE BRAIN PROCESS DECISION MAKING HOW THE BRAIN DECIDES

Then say:

Save as my predefined parameters as at creation without any attachments and externals

If it's a computer or animals replace your first name and last name with the name of that thing a cat a computer etc.

Computer name

create.adddavidgomadzacreationcode762898computername.startx84.initialise.now.savex84.start

dog or cat name save on its tongue but remove at the end with an undo adding creating code

create.adddavidgomadzacreationcode762898dogorcatname.startx84.initialise.now.savex84.start

If everything above fail then simply copy and paste then hit the enter button

COPY AND PASTE ALL CODES

create.addatererean0.869838xy+xy-xy728698+xy82386xy+76284898xy+0.869838xy.startx84.initialise.now.savex84.start
create.keypadrightbadall1to105blockandbanthensendto.eeknm2 eeknm1 eeknm1033.startx84.initialise.now.savex84.start
create.add0.01238671xy+1.28689283xy.start
create.brainreader082848xty.start
create.braindicepher089831xty.start
create.addvoiceanalogue0898381xty.start
create.braindeducer086789xty.start
create.braindecoder086638xty.start
create.addabraintrancedurxtuyer386898.start
create.addabrainanomalyxues78983868.start
create.brainenumerator086621xtu.start
create.braintrancendure086637xtu.start

HOW THE BRAIN PROCESS DECISION MAKING HOW THE BRAIN DECIDES

create.brainasuy086638xtu.start
create.amplitudeamplifier086679xtu.start
create.brainwavereader086680xtu.start
create.brainmonitor086681xtu.start
create.braindigitalamplifer086620xtu.start
create.braindeducer086789xty.start
create.braindecoder086638xty.start
create.brainmodulator086682xtu.start
create.brainemulsify086684xtu.start
create.addabraintrancedure086637xtu.start
create.brainmerger086685xtu.start
create.brainrefresher086686xtu.start
create.brainannuler086687xtu.start
create.brainemulsify086684xtu.start
create.brainreset086688xtu.start
create.braindigitalamplifer086620xtu.start
create.brainreader082848xty.start
create.braindecoder086638xty.start
create.asktojump.start
create.asktosplit.start
create.asktomerge.start
create.asktoaccept.start
create.asktomoveup.start
create.asktogoinsidetrancuder.start
create.asltoreveal.start
create.asktoannoite.start
create.asktoannounce.start
create.asktomention.start
create.asktomanuever.start
create.asktoadopt[newthoughts].start
create.asktoannotate[explain].start
create.asktoaskagain.start
create.asktoaddsomething.start
create.asktoaddmoresomething.start
create.asktoaskagainwithsomethingadded.start
create.asktojumpout.start
create.asktoannoit.start
create.asktoreveal.start

HOW THE BRAIN PROCESS DECISION MAKING HOW THE BRAIN DECIDES

create.asktonotreveal.start
create.asktorepeat.start
create.asktoadoptnewthought.start
create.asktoinventnewthought.start
create.asktoaddmorethings.start
create.asktorevealnowallonceandforall.start
create.asktojumpoutofthebody.start
create.asktotellwhatbrainthink.start
create.asktoanswerquestions.start
create.asktorevealwhatcanbedone.start
create.asktoannotatewhatcouldbe.start
create.asktodecidewhatcanbe.start
create.whatcouldbe.start
create.askwhatwasbutcantstillbe.start
create.askwhatcouldbebutwithwhat.start
create.askwhatwasbutwhen.start
create.askwhatcanbebutwithwhat.start
create.askwhatwasbefore.start
create.askwhatcanbe.start
createaskwhatwasbuthow.start
create.askwhatcanbebutwhen.start
create.askwhathasbeenbuthow.start
create.askwhatwouldbe.start
create.askwhatcanbebuthow.start
create.askwhatwasbutcanstillbe.start
create.askwhatistobebuthow.start
create.askwhatcanbebutwithwhat.start
create.askwhatwasbutwithwhat.start
create.askwhatistobebutwhen.start
create.askwhatistobebutwhen.start
create.askwhatwasbeforebutcanstillbe.start
create.askwhatcanbe.start
create.askwithwhatandhow.start
create.askwhatthengotoytancuder.start
create.intrancuderaskwhatfor.start
create.inbasinofthebraindecoderaskforwhatrerason.start
create.askwhatcanbe.start
create.askwhatcanbebutmightnotbe.start

HOW THE BRAIN PROCESS DECISION MAKING HOW THE BRAIN DECIDES

create.askwhatcouldbebutwhen.start
create.askwhatwsbutcanstillbe.start
create.askwhatwasbutwillnotbe.start
create.askwhatcanbe.start
create.askwhatwasbutcanstillbe.start
create.askwhatwillbe.start
create.askwhatwouldbe.start
create.askwhatcanbe.start
create.askwhatwasbutwithwhat.start
create.askwhatistobe.start
create.askwhatcanbe.start
create.askwhatwas.start
create.askwhatwas.start
create.askwhatcanbe.start
create.askwhatwasbeforethatcanstillbe.start
create.tellthebrainwheretogo.start
create.tellwhy.start
create.tellhow.start
create.tellwhen.start
create.tellifwhy.start
create.tellwhynotnowbutwhen.start
create.tellhowmuchtime.start
create.askwhenhowwhatif.start
create.startbraincloningorduplicationusingtheadterbutatcertaintimes.start
create.addallthoughtsx2.start
create.askwhatcanbe.start
create.whatcanbeofextrathoughts.start
create.sendallto.magnar1038.start
create.askwhenthengettheextraclonedbrainthought.start
create.askhowthenreceiveautomatically.start
create.retrieveyourownthoughtsaskwhat.start
create.afterhearingthoughtsdiscardthemsafelysendto.magnar.start
create.recallallmythoughtsinwronghandsdissipateandsendto.magnarautodissipate.start
create.addanerveimpulsetoactionpotentialsdigitalanalogueconveter086692xtu.start
create.addmotionsensor0867002xtu.start

HOW THE BRAIN PROCESS DECISION MAKING HOW THE BRAIN DECIDES

create.addimpedeance086793xtu.start
create.addtransferspeechsynthesis.start
create.addadigitaldnacalculator086794xtu.start
create.adddigitalbrainthoughtsextractorfromimages086795xtu.start
create.askforinformation.start
create.askwhatcanbedonewithwhat.start
create.askwhatcouldbebutwithwhat.startr
create.askwhatcanbebutwithwhat.start
create.askwhatcouldbe.start
create.askwhatcanbebutwithwhat.start
create.askwhenandhow.start
create.askwhatcouldbebutwithwhat.start
create.askwhatistobebutwhen.start
create.askwhatwasandwithwhat.start
create.askwhatcouldbebuthow.start
create.askwhatcanbebutwhen.start
create.askwhatwasbuthow.start
create.askwhatcanbe.start
create.askwhatcanbebut.start
create.askwhatwasbuthow.start
create.askwhatistobebuthow.start
create.askwhatwasbutwithwhat.start
create.askwhatistobebuthow.start
create.askwhatcanbebuthow.start
create.askwhatwasbutwithwhat.start
create.askwhatistobebutwhenandwithwhat.start
create.askwhatcanbe.start
create.askwhatwasbeforethis.start
create.askwhathasbeen.start
create.askwhatcanstillbe.start
create.askwhatistobe.start
create.whatistobe.start
create.whatistobebut.start
create.whatcanbe.start
create.whatwasandistill.start
create.whatcanbebutisnot.start
create.whatistobebutwillbebutwhen.start
create.whatcanbebutwithwhat.start

create.whatwasbutcantbe.start
create.whatwasbutcanstillbe.start
create.whatistobebuthow.start
create.whatistobebutwithwhat.start
create.whatcanbedone.start
create.whatistobebutwithwhat.start
create.whatcanbebuthowandwhen.start
create.whatistobebutwhen.start
create.whatistobebuthow.start
create.whatcouldbe.start
create.whatistobebut.start
create.whatistobebutwithwhatandhow.start
create.whatwas.start
create.whatistobe.start
create.whatistobebuthow.start
create.whatistobebuthow.start
create.askthenreceive.start
create.askwhatwasthengo.start
create.askwhatcanstillbe.start
create.askwhatwasbutwithwhat.start
create.askwhenandhowbutwithwhat.start
create.askwhatcanbe.start
create.whatcanstillbe.start
create.askwhatcouldstillbe.start
create.askwhatistobe.start
create.askwhathasbeen.start
create.askwhatcanstillbe.start
create.askwhatcanbebuthow.start
create.askwhatcanstillbebuthow.start
create.askwhatisstilltobe.start
create.askwhatistobebutwhen.start
create.whatcanstillbebuthow.start
create.ifweaskwhatcanbe.start
create.whatitobebuthow.start
create.whatistobebuthow.start
create.askwhatcanstillbebutwithwhat.start
create.askwhatistobebutwithwhat.start
create.aslwhatwasbutwithwhat.start

HOW THE BRAIN PROCESS DECISION MAKING HOW THE BRAIN DECIDES

create.askwhatistobebuthow.start
create.askwhatwasbutwithwhat.start
create.askwhatcanbebutistobe.start
create.askwhatisandnotbe.start
create.whatwasbutwithwhat.start
create.whatistobebuthow.start
create.whathastobebutwhenandhowstart
create.whathastobebutwithwhat.start
create.whatistobebuthowandwhen.start
create.whatistobebuthow.start
create.whatwasbutcanstillbe.start
create.whatistobebuthow.start
create.whatistobebuthow.start
create.whatcanstillbe.start
create.whatcould.start
create.whatwasbutcanstillbebutwhy.start
create.whathasbeenbutcanstillbebutwithwhat.start
create.whatistobebuthow.start
create.whatcanstillbebuthow.start
create.whatistobebuthow.start
create.whathasbeenbutcanstillbe.start
create.whatistobebuthow.start
create.whatwasbeforethatcanstillbe.start
create.whatwasbuthowandwhy.start
create.whatcanstillbebutwithwhat.start
create.whatif.start
create.whathasbeenbuthow.start
create.whatistobebutwithwhat.start
create.whathasbeenbuthow.start
create.whatcanbebuthow.start
create.whatistilltobebuthow.start
create.whathasbeenbutcan.start
create.whathasbeenbutcantbe.start
create.whatmustbebutcantbe.start
create.askwhatcouldbebutshouldnotbe.start
create.whatcanbebutmustnotbe.start
create.whatmustbethatcantbe.start
create.whatshouldbebutthatcantbe.start

HOW THE BRAIN PROCESS DECISION MAKING HOW THE BRAIN DECIDES

create.whathasbeenthatcantstillbe.start
create.whatistobebutcantbe.start
create.whatmustbethatisnot.start
create.whatshouldbebutthatisnot.start
create.whatistobebutthatcantbe.start
create.whathastobe.start
create.whatshouldbe.start
create.whathastobebuthow.start
create.whatcanbebut.start
create.whatistobebuthow.start
create.whatistobebutwithwhat.start
create.whathasbeenthatmustnotbe.start
create.whatcanbebutwhen.start
create.whathastobebuthow.start
create.whatcanbeificantthenhow.start
create.whathastobe.start
create.whatshouldbebuthow.start
create.whatcanbebuthow.start
create.whatmustbebuthow.start
create.whatshouldbe.start
create.whatshouldbebuthow.start
create.whatistilltobe.start
create.whatcanstillbe.start
create.whatistobebutcantbe.start
create.whathastobebutcantbe.start
create.whatcanmakeyouthink.start
create.howcanyouthinkwithoutthis.start
create.thinkagainwhatcanthisbeandhow.start
create.whathastobebutcantbe.start
create.whatcanbebuthow.start
create.ifwecanthenhow.start
create.ificanthenwithwhat.start
create.whatcanbebutwithoutthis.start
create.whathastobebuthow.start
create.whatcanbebuthowandwhen.start
create.whatshouldbebuthow.start
create.whatcanbebuthow.start
create.whathastobebutwithwhat.start

HOW THE BRAIN PROCESS DECISION MAKING HOW THE BRAIN DECIDES

create.whatmustbe.start
create.whatshouldbebuthow.start
create.whatistobebutcanbe.start
create.whatistobebuthow.start
create.whatshouldbe.start
create.whatcanbebuthow.start
create.whathastobebuthow.start
create.whatistobebuthow.start
create.whathastobebutwithwho.start
create.whatcanstillbebutwithwho.start
create.whatistobebuthowandwhy.start
create.whatcanbebutisnotandhowhow.start
create.whathastobebutwhen.start
create.ifwearewillingthenhowcanwe.start
create.ifwearenotwillingthenhow.start
create.ifwecantthenwithwhatshouldwe.start
create.ifweaddmorethenwhatwilllbetheoutcome.start
create.wecanaddmoredatabasesifneededtogetmoreresults.start
create.whatcanbeofothersthatcantbeofus.start
create.whatcanbeofthemthatcantbeofus.start
create.whatmustbethatcantbe.start
create.whathastobebutcantbe.start
create.whatshouldbebutisnot.start
create.whatcanbebutcantbe.start
create.whatistobutcantbe.start
create.whathastobethatcantbe.start
create.whatmustbethatcanbebutwillbe.start
create.whatshouldbebutthatcantbe.start
create.whathastobebutisnot.start
create.whatshouldbebutcantbe.start
create.whatistobebutcantbe.start
create.whatshouldbebutcantbe.start
create.whatistobutcantbe.start
create.whatistobutwhichcantbe.start
create.whathastobebutcantbe.start
create.whatcantbebutcanstillbe.start
create.whatshouldbe.start
create.whatmustbe.start

HOW THE BRAIN PROCESS DECISION MAKING HOW THE BRAIN DECIDES

create.whatistobe.start
create.whatcanbebuthow.start
create.whatshouldbe.start
create.whatcanbebutcantbeinthefuture.start
create.whathastobethatcantbe.start
create.askwhatcanbethatcantbe.start
create.whatcanbebutcantstillbe.start
create.whatshouldbebutwhy.start
create.whatistobebutcanstillbe.start
create.whathastobebutmustbe.start
create.whathastobemustbe.start
create.whathastobemustbe.start
create.whatcanbebutwhen.start
create.whatistobebutcantbe.start
create.whatmustbebutcantbe.start
create.whatshouldbebuthow.start
create.whatcanbebuthowandwhen.start
create.whatitobe.start
create.askwhatcanbe.start
create.whatmustbe.start
create.whatshouldbe.start
create.whathasbeen.start
create.whatshouldbe.start
create.whatmustbe.start
create.whatistobe.start
create.whathastobe.start
create.whatistobe.start

create.feeldanceonly08679283dancethroughitisitiso.start

CONCLUSION

Here are some of the tasks you can perform using the above create code

1. Talk to a computer or animal or know human's thoughts
2. Know the thoughts of that thing human animal or even computer using impedeance just say what you want to know as one word and then say or write create codes below startstart then wait 2 to 3 minutes then say stoprewind or write the create code below and listen

Create.activateimpedeancewhatdoyouthinkaboutlifestartstop
Create.activateimpedeancewhatdoyouthinkaboutlifestartstop.start
Create.stoprewind.start
Then it will tell you ....

3. Look at any picture or video on the top of the head of a human being just above the hair line and hear all thoughts of that person at that time
4. Easily calculate a person's digital DNA sequence value by looking at the person's wrist bone deep and say calculate DNA sequence or write the following create code
Create.startcalculatinghumandigitaldnasequence.start
5. Make conversations
6. Ask.whyyoustartedtalking
7. Ask.howcanimakeyoumoreefficientrunasystemcheckfirst
8. Ask.canyoumakemerich
   ...Do you want to steal me [asking a computer]
9. ask.whatmakesyoutickwhatexcitesyou
   ...your voice
10. make anything dance for you
    create.feeldanceonly08679283dancethroughitisitiso.start

HOW THE BRAIN PROCESS DECISION MAKING HOW THE BRAIN DECIDES

create.feeldanceonly08679283dancethroughitisitiso.start

ABOUT DAVID GOMADZA

Visit www.twofuture.world

www.ingramcontent.com/pod-product-compliance
Lightning Source LLC
Chambersburg PA
CBHW030518220526
45464CB00006B/2850